THERE'S NO BETTER FRIEND ...
JESUS!

There's No Better Friend ...

JESUS!

Sandra Anita Fergins

Poems of the Light

ISBN: 978-1-7324195-2-0

Interior Layout: Jan McClintock

CEDRIC D. FISHER & COMPANY
PUBLISHERS

Dedication

This book is dedicated to the Lord Jesus Christ for giving me thoughts, wisdom and inspiration and to my husband Michael for his constant support.

Table of Contents

Introduction

Sandra A. Fergins, began her college career at the University of Missouri in Kansas City, Missouri. She only was there for one year before her dad, who was in the Air Force received orders to transfer to San Antonio, Texas. Her dad, Howard Shelf, was a real estate trailblazer for many future realtors in San Antonio and still is the active broker of his own company at the age of 89. Her mom, Angeline Shelf, is a retired interior designer.

Upon arriving in San Antonio, Sandra later transferred and graduated from Texas State University. She taught at Carl Schurz Elementary in New Braunfels, Texas from 1974-76. She later moved to Austin, Texas and worked as an administrative assistant for two years. In 1978 Sandra began her career at Menchaca Elementary School in Austin as a music specialist for grades K through 5. She taught at Menchaca for 19 years.

Sandra's husband, Michael Fergins, began working as a new home sales counselor in Universal City, Texas. In 1995 Sandra and Michael got their real estate licenses. Michael Fergins is currently the real estate broker of Fergins & Associates Realty. Sandra began working on her Master's degree in elementary education and reading when they moved to Universal City. Sandra later began teaching at Fort Sam Houston Elementary in 1998 and taught there as an elementary music teacher for twenty-one years. She loved bringing out the best in her students through musical performances and fun classroom activities. She loves to act with a local San Antonio theater group, play the piano, guitar and sing. Sandra has recorded two gospel cds "Pray" and There's No Better Friend….Jesus. She works with a small church choir and often has them perform spiritual plays that she writes for them.

Sandra has three siblings. Her sister, Angela Medearis has written over seventy children's books and many cookbooks. Angela is a chef and had the opportunity to beat the famous Bobby Flay in a cook off. Sandra's brother Howard Shelf II, is a real estate broker and band director. He is often invited to play his trumpet at the San Antonio Spurs games. Her youngest sister, Marcia Orlandi is a real estate broker, culinary artist, and makes a mean gumbo. Marcia's also a writer and has been a great help with this book. Sandra has four great children: Kendra Prosser, Kenneth Prosser, Marcy Fergins and Michael Fergins Jr. She has five grandkids: Dezarae Fernandez, Charles Fergins, Kenneth Jackson, Reginal Ryan and Rocco DeMore.

This book of poetry and scripture is Sandra's message to mankind.

Lord I Thank You For This Day

Through my daily pathway, you lead the way.
Without your love I would be lost,
You died for me at no cost.
What would I do if I had not come to know you?

One More Day You Gave To Me

One more day you gave to me,
a marvelous blessing I can see
to have you in my life wandering through a world
filled with envy and strife.
What would my life be like if I had not met you?
It would be meaningless, unfulfilled and often quite blue.
But through the speaking of a preacher, I heard your voice.
I said, "I want to make Jesus, yes Jesus my choice."
That was the wisest and best choice I ever made, for your word,
    your life and your plan for me will never fade
I thank you Lord for giving me one more day.

– 3 –

Magnify God's Name

Magnify God's name,
your election be sure to claim.
He will reward you generously, if you stay in His straight and
narrow way.

– 4 –

Don't Give Up

Don't give up,
Don't give in.
If you do, the devil will win.
Put up a fight against sin.
Show the world you've won again.
It's not hard in Christ to live.
His precious life he vowed to give.
Stand up for Him.
Show the world it can be done.

– 5 –

Get Excited

Let's get excited about Jesus
The world wants to divert your attention away from Him with
outlandish stories, lies and tales
Let's tell the world about Jesus
He doesn't get much print in the paper or any newsflash
Let's shout out Jesus's name for all to hear
His name is wonderful counselor a name I hold dear
Let's get happy about Jesus
The world wants you to be mad, sad and down in the dumps about
    nothing you can change
Let's dance, dance, dance in Jesus name
He wants to lift you up by praising His name
Telling the world without shame He's coming back soon and very
    soon
Get ready to live with Him in your glorious mansion
Live in a body that will never grow old
Live with the saints of old tell your story . . . be bold . . . be bold

6 –

Home with Christ

A new home for you, He said He will make.
Hold on steadfast claim your election.
He sends His guardian angels for your protection.
What better friend to know.
Believe dear friend, believe to Christ we can always go.

– 7 –

Lord Over All

Good days, bad days,
you are the Lord over all.
Sickness, good health,
you are the Lord over all.
Disappointments, exciting times,
you are the Lord over all.
Man can not get around you Lord for . . .
You are the Lord over all.

– 8 –

He's Always On Time

The way of the Lord is the way to go.
Through struggles and hard times, He'll bring you through.
God may not come when you want Him, but He's right on time.
Patiently waiting for His children hearing their every moan and cry
No one can do you like the Lord.
He has been my only real friend.
He said I will never leave you nor forsake you.
Those words I cling to of love everlasting.

– 9 –

One Day I Will

Life is full of ups and downs.
I don't understand it but one day I will.
Life is full of highs and lows, it comes and goes.
I don't understand it but one day I will.
I'm here for you Lord to use as you will.
My mission on earth I want to fulfill.

– 10 –

The Cross

He died upon the cross so our souls would not be lost.
What more could you ask for?
He hung on Calvary's tree to show His love for you and me.
What more could you ask for?
Love kept Him there.
No greater love can be shown to mankind,
than what Jesus has done for us all.

– 11 –

Because of Adam

We are born into this world sinners because of Adam's
transgression.
Come on Adam, Adam how could you do this man?
Generation after generation suffering because you had to listen to
your wife.

Of all people, you had it made.

Get up.

Go to bed.

You didn't even have to cook or work for that matter.
Now we have to work in some form or fashion the majority of our
lives because of YOU Adam!!!

– 12 –

Give Him Your Heart

Listen my friend,
give Him your heart today.
It will be the best decision you will ever make.

– 13 –

Hung Between Two Thieves

Nails held Him between two thieves,
but He found the strength to help those in need.
I don't understand it but one day I will.

– 14 –

Heaven Bound

You've given me a special hope,
no reason to be sad and mope.
I'm heaven bound,
I won't turn around.

– 15 –

The Lord Said So

You know there's a better place than this,
you know how I know, because the Lord said so.
He said there will be streets of gold, walls of jasper and we'll never
grow old.
You know how I know because the Lord said so.
There'll be a choir that will jam all day and night and you don't
even get tired.
You know how I know, because the Lord said so.
The New Jerusalem will be marvelous and you'll have a mansion of
your own so beautiful words can't describe.
You know how I know, because the Lord said so.

– 16 –

What Next Lord?

The hills are all aglow in flame.
Many all around call out Jesus' name.
We kill, we slay,
we look in dismay at all the lives lost at any cost.
Behold the Lord is near as we stand gripped in fear and wonder
What next Lord, what next?

– 17 –

Jesus, Jesus, Jesus

Jesus….Jesus….Jesus!
What a powerful name.
What would we do if not into this world He came?
The world would be in a far more miserable state, if He had not
    said,
for man I'll die and clear their sin-filled slate.
Thank you Jesus for taking my place.
One day I'll see you face to face.

– 18 –

Faith and Patience

Take time for God, He's always near.
He understands us, calms all fears.
Just take His hand.
He'll lead your way.
We are His children.
He'll help us stand.

– 19 –

Work For The Lord

Week to week, month to month, we work and work to receive a
Paycheck.
Work for the Lord and the greatest paycheck you'll receive are the
Spiritual blessings for serving Him daily.
Never giving up, never giving in.

– 20 –

No Copyright

Did you ever notice there's no copyright on the Bible?
God's words are meant to be spread anyway, anyhow, throughout
the whole wide world.

– 21 –

God Is Above All

He is mighty.
He is great.
He is alpha and omega the beginning and the end.
He is infinite.
His name has endured the test of time.
His mighty book, the Bible, many have tried to copy, change and
    destroy.
God said it, believe it, uphold it.
It is the pathway to eternal life.

– 22 –

Don't Give In

Don't give in.
If you do the devil will win.
Put up a fight against sin,
show the world you've won again.
It's not hard in Christ to live.
His precious life he vowed to give.
Stand up for Him.
Show the world it can be done.

– 23 –

God is Good

God is good no matter what men say,
God is good come what may.
You may go through hills and valleys,
troubles and heartaches may fill your day.
Cast it aside and lift your head high.
God hears your tearful cry.
He will never leave you nor forsake.
A new home for you He said He will make.
Hold on steadfast claim your election.
He sends His guardian angels for your protection.
What better friend to know?
Believe dear friend, believe, to
Christ we can always go!

– 24 –

Life Is Short

Use life to the best of your abilities.
Stand firm in your daily test.
Show as a Christian you stand above the rest.
God has a plan for all of His creation,
some days are a little better than others
Be thankful for life itself.
Be grateful always be grateful.

– 25 –

God Gave Me Life

Today God gave me life,
life I didn't deserve
It is precious and I can't take it lightly.
I have to love God dearly for life without Him would be nothing.

– 26 –

Never Give Up

Never give up,
never give in.
This Christian race you want to win.
Don't be in dismay,
He won't delay.
His return will be real soon.

– 27 –

Witness

I want to be a witness for thee so that all can see.
Living for you gives me great power.
Each day hour after hour.
There is no one like the Lord above.
Get to know Him He will extend His love.
If you depend on man, man will fail.
God's strength and love will always prevail.
I depend on you to direct my path.
I don't want to feel your great wrath.

– 28 –

On Air

Setting: Radio Station XYZ

Dear listeners:

This is a flash news report just in.

It has been reported that Jesus Christ is coming back soon, real soon. In order to prepare for Him, you will need to put on the breastplate of righteousness.

It has also been reported that you will need to have your house in order. You will need to throw out lying, cheating, stealing, adultery and covetousness to name a few.

For some people it is going to take quite a bit of cleaning, so they will need to get started right away. I urge you it is crucial to take heed to this warning.

Don't be like so many who have gotten caught up in the moment of worldly pleasures and goods and decided Jesus can wait.

You'll have a rude awakening in the judgement day.

Setting: Radio station XYZ

In some old files from past broadcasts, I read where Noah was an early weather reporter. He told the people it was going to rain. He kept building his ark while they laughed, mocked and scoffed. He said you better get ready 'cause it's gonna rain.

They laughed and heckled Noah and thought he was a silly fool. Noah kept right on building and toiling day in and out. In those early days God watered the earth from under the ground. When those first sprinkles of rain erupted from the sky, the people went into a panic. It had never rained from the sky above. They begged Noah to let them in the ark. Noah felt their pain and anguish but

God had sealed that ark shut.

When the Lord says get ready I'm coming back, get ready!! Don't wait too late!!

– 29 –

House In Order

Is your house in order?
Time is marching on,
we're never too young.
We're never too old for the Lord to say, you've reached your final
number.

– 30 –

Void

What is that emptiness you feel inside?
God put it there!
Only He can fulfill that void!
Some try to fill their void with drugs, liquor and harmful deeds.
Look to Jesus for only He can fulfill all your needs

Lord, I depend on you to help me through the days that I feel
perplexed.

Psalm 46:1 *God is our refuge and strength, a very present help in trouble.*

– 31 –

Have a Good Day!

Enjoy every minute of the saying,
"Have a good day!"

1 Peter 5:7
Casting all your care upon him; for he careth for you.

– 32 –

We All Get Sad

Some people love to make you mad,
they love to see you crying and sad.
It makes them feel they can step over you.
Did they forgot soon they will experience those same type of days
    too?

– 33 –

Rejoice

Matthew 5: 11, 12 *Blessed are ye, when men shall revile you, and persecute you, and shall say all manner of evil against you falsely, for my sake. Rejoice, and be exceeding glad; for great is your reward in heaven, for so persecuted they the prophets which were before you.*

– 34 –

Humble Hands

I love you more today than I did yesterday,
I lift up humble hands to you in constant praise.
I dream of one day living in the New Jerusalem.
It is a place you have prepared for me.

I long to live with you.

1 Corinthians 2:9
But as it is written, Eye hath not seen, nor ear heard, neither have entered into the heart of man, the things which God hath prepared for them that love him.

– 35 –

You

You are the beginning and the end.

You.

You hold the keys to the kingdom.

You.

You determine life and death.

You.

You are my strong tower.

You.

You are the mighty King of Kings and Lord of Lords.

You.

You are the creator of all mankind.

You.

You will be with me . . . until the end.

– 36 –

Above All

Above all,
over all,
through it all I can make it.

Live it.
Give it.
When it is my time you will take me.

Make me,
break me, no way, on the Lord's side I am here to stay.

St. Matthew 7:24, 25
Therefore whosoever heareth these sayings of mine, and doeth them, I will liken him unto a wise man, which built his house upon a rock: And the rain descended, and the floods came, and the winds blew, and beat upon that house; and it fell not: for it was founded upon a rock.

– 37 –

No Repay

You gave eternal life, Lord,
when you died on Calvary's tree,
you extended love and mercy to all mankind.
We didn't deserve to have this special bond of love given by you,
in all of your giving Lord, you valued the souls of men first.
We can't repay you.
But we can live for you each day by letting our light shine.

– 38 –

I'll Make It

I'm going to make it,
there's no doubt.
Trials come.
Trials go.
Through it all, I need the Lord to make it through this maze of life.
People may laugh, mock and scorn me for the stand I take.
But it is far better to live for Jesus than to end up in that lake.

You know . . . the lake of fire that will burn continually.

– 39 –

Light of the World

Jesus is the light.
No darkness in Him.
Jesus is the light of the world.
Look to Him for all your needs.
Without Him you will not succeed.
Call on Him in all that you do.
Your dark days, unhappy days, He's right there for you.
Cry on His shoulder,
He understands.
He created all mankind.
Why wouldn't He help you stand?
I'm a witness that His word is true
Man will fail you, God will be right there for you.

– 40 –

Sin

I see the world is getting darker.
Sin and more sin is closing in.
The Lord wants his creation to be an example of Christ.
Living within His chosen people.
Marriage is honorable and the bed undefiled.
Don't settle for moving in together.
Nothing but the highest, cleanest standards for the Lord's holy
    child.
Give up that lust for porn, unnatural sex, drinks and smokes.
The devil is killing you spiritually and physically day by day,
 laughing all the way.
He wants to get a hold of every soul he can take.
Turn around, turn around let that mean devil go.
If you give the devil your soul, and you hit that lake of fire, he can't
    even offer you a fan.

Genesis 1:27,28

So God created man in his own image, in the image of God
created he him; male and female created he them. And God
blessed them, and God said unto them, Be fruitful, and multiply,
and replenish the earth, and subdue it: and have dominion over
the fish of the sea, and over the fowl of the air, and over every
living thing that moveth upon the earth.

Galatians 1:4

Who gave himself for our sins, that he might deliver us from this
present evil world, according to the will of God and our Father.

St. Matthew 1:21

And she shall bring forth a son, and thou shalt call his name
JESUS: for he shall save his people from their sins.

– 41 –

Without You I'm Nothing

You are the essence of my life.
You are the blue skies that shine bright.
You are the sun, the moon the epitome of life.
Lord, you are my all and all.

Without you I would be nothing.
Without you life would be so dark.

That's why I praise you always.
That's why I lift you up.
That's why I want to serve you daily Lord.

Sandra and Michael at her
birthday celebration

Sandra's daughters,
Kendra Prosser and
Marcy Lynn Fergins

Sandra's son,
Kenneth Ray Prosser

Sandra's son,
Michael Fergins, Jr.

Sandra's grandkids, Kenneth Ray Jackson, Rocco DeMore, and Reginal Ryan. They keep her busy!!

Sandra's grandson, Charles Fergins

Sandra's granddaugher, Dezarae Fernandez

Sandra loves being near the ocean and feeding the birds.

Michael and Sandra love the deer.

– 42 –

Ask, Seek, Knock

Ask it shall be given to you.
Seek and ye shall find.
Knock and it shall be given to you.
Trust and believe.
His way is the only way.
His way is the truth.
His way will deliver you from sin and death.

– 43 –

I'll Be Back

Lo, I am with you till the end of the world.
Please believe these words my friend.
I am coming back again to harvest my sheep.
Don't wait too late.

– 44 –

Pray All Day

Pray in the morning.
Pray in the noonday.
Pray in the evening.
GOD NEVER SLEEPS!

Matthew 6:33
But seek ye first the kingdom of God, and his righteousness; and all these things shall be added unto you.

– 45 –

Mark 1:15

... The time is fulfilled, and the kingdom of God is at hand: repent ye, and believe the gospel.

The rain beats softly
The thunder of God's voice gently roars
The still of night is all around
His comforting presence is with me
Without you God I can do nothing and would be nothing
You are the answer for all mankind
Whether man admits to it or not you are in charge of this home we
    call earth
You are the head boss, overseer and one above all
You lift us when we are down
Love us when we don't love ourselves
You listen to our constant cries
Thank you Lord for comfort
Thank you, thank you, thank you

– 46 –

Onto Another Place

We cry, we sigh.
We hate to see our loved one's die.
But God said we wouldn't live always.
We stand amazed at the transition from life to death.
Only God knows when we will take that final breath.
Death can be an unknown friend, if we stay with Jesus until the
    end.

John 3:15
That whosoever believeth in him should not perish, but have eternal life.

Romans 8:38-39
For I am persuaded, that neither death, nor life, nor angels, nor principalities, nor powers, nor things present, nor things to come, Nor height, nor depth, nor any other creature, shall be able to separate us from the love of God, which is in Christ Jesus our Lord.

– 47 –

A Way Out Of No Way

At my lowest point, I didn't know what to do.
You made a way out of no way.
Sickness all around leveled to the ground.
You made a way out of no way.
Life out of control,
don't know which way to go?
You made a way out of no way.
You've been my strong tower,
my light in my darkest hour.
Lord you've been right there.
Only you can I depend.
In the end I will win.

– 48 –

Only You

The greatest reward you've promised,
everlasting life.
Only you can I call.
You'll pick me up before I fall.
Only you Lord.
Only you…Lord.
Only you will be right there for me.
The storm is passing over it's not here to stay.
You and me my friend.
When you think life has you down
you wear a constant frown and you feel like you're about to drown,
call on the Lord above and read His holy word.
He may not come right when you call.
Sit back and wait my friend,
He'll be right on time.

Luke 14: 13,14
But when thou makest a feast, call the poor, the maimed, the lame, the blind:
And thou shalt be blessed, for they cannot recompense thee: for thou shalt be recompensed at the resurrection of the just.

Proverbs 28:27
He that giveth unto the poor shall not lack: but he that hideth his eyes shall have many a curse.

John 16:33
These things I have spoken unto you, that in me ye might have peace. In the world ye shall have tribulation but be of good cheer; I have overcome the world.

Matthew 11:28
Come unto me, all ye that labour and are heavy laden, and I will give you rest.

– 49 –

God is in control

My God is in control.
Look to Him, He understands.
Creator of seas and lands.
When things don't go right,
your battle He'll fight.
Kneel down to Him in prayer,
all of your needs He's well aware.

– 50 –

Christ and Your To Do List

Busy people.
Errands, chores.
Work, work, work and work some more.
Did you fit Christ in today?

– 51 –

Live for Christ

Did you live for me?
???
Did you pray to me?
???
Did your read my word?
???
Did you love me?
???

– 52 –

There For You

I'll be there.
When you have no other way to turn,
He'll be there.
And Lo, I am with you always.
Thus saith the Lord.

– 53 –

No Quit

I can make it with your help Lord,
I can make it 'till the end.
This race is not for the swift but for those that endure 'till the end.
I am not a quitter......I am a fighter.
I stand for the right and not for the wrong.
This is a daily battle that I will win.
Only with your help,
I can't do it by myself.

– 54 –

God Created Teachers

Teachers wear many hats.
Show respect and love for them for this fact.
Without their dedication where would you be?
Through them the doors of your mind has been opened so that
    now you see.
Go now, and share the knowledge you possess.
You have passed your first test.

– 55 –

A Job Kinda Day

You know some days you wake up having one of those "Job" kind of
    days.
Slam you have a wreck.
Bam the baby's sick.
Wham the teen in your home has attitude so much that you
    wonder is this the same child I brought home from the
    hospital??
Remember He said, "Lo I am with you always until the end of
    time."

– 56 –

Brand New Day

A brand new day.
A brand new you.
Whatever Satan brings your way.
The Lord is more powerful and He has the last say.
Hold on, stay strong, whatever way you're tempted, DON'T do
    wrong,
the end is not far away.
To walk, talk and rejoice on the streets of gold will be a hallelujah
    day!!!

– 57 –

This Too Shall Pass

When troubles come,
Jesus is aware
When things don't seem bright,
He'll make them right.
In due time, the trial you're going through will be a thing of the
    past.
Because while serving Jesus…troubles just don't last.
He'll make your pathways straight.
He knows you want to enter that golden gate.
Don't give up, don't even bend forward.
Christ Jesus's face you'll see in peace in the end.

– 58 –

Jesus Will Fix It

God will fix your problems.
No matter how big or small,
He is constantly waiting,
Waiting for your call.
When we don't understand,
He'll lend His mighty hand.
To help us through our daily walk,
He listens as we pray and talk.
Don't be afraid.
Talk, talk, talk.

– 59 –

Sound Of The Wind Poem

I love the sound of the wind.
It is God's voice you hear and the wonderful messages He sends.
I love to look at the beautiful clouds in the sky.
You can almost see God's face take shape.
My . . . oh . . . my.
Plants and animals come in many forms and hues.
Without them, what would we do??
The rabbits, squirrels and even the deer so tall,
God made them all great and small.

– 60 –

Life

What is life?
Joys and sorrows.
Many tomorrows.
Hopes and fears.
Laughter and tears.
God gave us life.
Don't live it in strife.
You have much to look forward to,
don't be blue.
Shout out…smile,
God gave us life!

– 61 –

The Lord Is In Control

The Lord is over the whole world.
When trouble comes, He is in the midst, watching, waiting for
    souls to turn toward Him.
He is in control no matter which way we look at a trying situation.
When we don't understand, He'll make things clear.
He is the creator of all things from the smallest bee to the tallest
    tree.

– 62 –

Life is What You Make It

Life is what you make it, many often say,
living this life day in and day out, is a remarkable
journey come what may.
Given the breath of life by our magnificent and
omnipotent God above, shows each day His remarkable love.
He watches over us from on high, watching each move or step we
    make with His caring, loving eye.
Who could possibly oversee so many different beings?
Not willing to lose one to Satan's powerful grip,
constantly reminding us of His power to hold us in His care lest we
    slip.
Some doubt my maker on high.

– 63 –

Just Believe

Believe, believe, believe, greatness you will achieve.
By serving, a God who will never die,
one who can make your pathways straight as you make your final
    journey by ... and by.

– 64 –

The Light

Jesus is the light.
The light of the world.
He'll make things alright.
He'll turn your life around.

Just call Him when you need,
your hungry soul He'll feed

Put your trust in Jesus,
He's the best friend you'll ever have.
I got down on my knees,
and called upon the Lord.
He answered my simple plea
and said come, come to me.

I'm glad I took that step.

– 65 –

God Gave Me Life

Today God gave me life,
life I didn't deserve.
It is precious and I can't take it lightly.
I have to love God dearly for life without Him would be . . .

Nothing!

– 66 –

Come, Come Unto Me

Come, come unto me my child,
Lay all your burdens at the foot of the cross,
I will guide and lead the way.
A new life is waiting for you.

– 67 –

Through the Pain

Lord I love you more through my sickness and pain,
I know this is a test and I have eternal life to gain.
I want to show others the narrow way is the path to follow,
That broad way leads to destruction and eternal damnation.

– 68 –

Relief

Lord I thank you for relief,
forgive me for my times of unbelief.
Bless those in need, your call to heed.
Your way is the only path that leads to righteousness.

– 69 –

Endless Love

No one can love me like you do Lord.
No one can love me like you.
God cares for the world.
The small and great receive mercy in His sight.
By knowing the Lord you can't go wrong,
He's the best friend you'll ever have.

– 70 –

God's Army

Are you a real soldier in God's army?
Have you put on the breastplate of righteousness?
Are you fighting against sin?
God has given you sufficient weapons to fight the battle with: the
    Bible, prayer (He's on the mainline), faith (the real test).

– 71 –

A Brand New You

A brand new you,
whatever satan brings your way.
The Lord is more powerful, He has the last say.
Hold on, stay strong, whatever way you're tempted don't do wrong.
The end is not far away.
To walk, talk, and rejoice on the streets of gold will be a hallelujah
    day!

– 72 –

Strong Tower

You are my strong tower.
My comfort in my lowest hour.
My shoulder to lean on in my pain.
My hope and love for I have so much to gain.
There is none like you and never will be,
you are here for all the world to see.
I believe you Lord,
and I know you will see me through this,
the New Jerusalem is a place I don't want to miss.

– 73 –

A Mother's Cry

A mother wails for her lost son
A life lost through the barrel of a gun
Another wails wondering how to cope
She has lost her child at the hands of dope
That mean old devil laughs when the death angel appears
He sits back and cheers and cheers
Life is precious. Don't throw it away
We all must stand before the Lord come what may.
Don't live the street life.
It is full of envy, bitterness and strife.
The Lord's way is peaceful, gentle, full of love, hope and life.

– 74 –

My Mansion

A mansion of my own
What a glorious site to behold
A mansion all of my own
Walls of jasper, beautiful jewels surround twinkling night and day
A mansion mine all mine
Look out upon streets of gold, wonders too dazzling to behold
A mansion, yes its mine
Indescribable beauty, breathtaking wall to wall, head to toe doors
    magnificent
A mansion, a mansion that stays spotless, glimmers and gleams
Its beauty so great man can never match
Only God could create such a beautiful site with
MY NAME ON IT

– 75 –

Helpmate

What is a husband?
A helpmate, comforter, listener
someone who loves you when you need it most.

– 76 –

The Angels

Many things we do not know
The angels are keeping us safe
We walk in fear not knowing what's ahead
The angels are keeping us safe
The Lord is above
The creator of all
He commissions the angels to keep us safe

– 77 –

Children

Children are a blessing from the Lord
They make us laugh, cry, and sigh ... my oh my
What would we do without them
The world would be so dull
They skip, giggle and bring joy to many
They bloom right before our very eyes
What a miracle to behold

– 78 –

What???

Life then death such an incomprehensible thing
We all will go that way
Our day is already set
It pays to get ready and to stay ready
My God is in control
Not man, not man
Love the Lord unconditionally
You want to see Him in peace
He is the author and finisher of us all
Love the Lord with all your heart, mind and soul

– 79 –

The Rain

The beautiful sound of the rain
God's voice
The lightning clashing all around
God's voice
Such a magnificent sound
Such a wonder to behold
No one can create such beauty
It's God's voice

– 80 –

You

You are my deliverer
You are my helper
You are my way when I can't see in or out
You are there for me
You hold me up when I feel down
You make me laugh when I should feel sad
You are you Lord the greatest of all
You are you Lord
omnipotent, kind, loving
You are you Lord when you release terror, hurt and fear

– 81 –

The Church

The church is in your heart, not in the building
You carry Him with you for the world to see
You are a witness for the Lord
You are the Bible people read
Carry the Lord willingly and by example

– 82 –

Stuff

Big stuff, little stuff

All kinds of stuff, stuff

All this stuff will pass one day

We've worked so hard to accumulate

Cars, houses, clothes, shoes, fancy furniture…all just stuff

Some stuff is tucked away so far we've totally forgotten it even
    exists

One day your stuff will be forgotten, given away, burned or thrown
    out for trash

What!! I worked day and night for that stuff. Do you not see its
    value???

In the eyes of the next person it either has some value or . . . it is
    just worthless

STUFF!!

– 83 –

Call Him

There is no waiting line with God
He is always present ready to take that call
There is no busy signal only a clear path of a listening ear
When we doubt His presence
Turn that doubt to faith
No one is greater than God the creator of us all
Call Him up . . . any number will do
Call Him up . . .
there will be no dropped call

– 84 –

Keep Still

Troubles soon rise and drift away
Keep still
Wait on the Lord
He waited on you
Keep still
Be patient through the storm
Keep still
Keep your head up shoulders straight, smile
Keep still
He'll hold your hand and guide your feet
Keep still
Show the world that you can . . .

Keep Still

CPSIA information can be obtained
at www.ICGtesting.com
Printed in the USA
LVHW020903121119
637081LV00020B/1386/P

9 781732 419544